Multicultural Crafts
Kids Can Do!

Asian-American Crafts Kids Can Do!

Sarah Hartman

Enslow Elementary

an imprint of

Enslow Publishers, Inc.

40 Industrial Road   PO Box 38

Enslow Elementary, an imprint of Enslow Publishers, Inc.

Enslow Elementary® is a registered trademark of Enslow Publishers, Inc.

Library of Congress Cataloging-in-Publication Data

Hartman, Sarah.
    Asian-American crafts kids can do! / Sarah Hartman.
        p. cm. — (Multicultural crafts kids can do!)
    Includes bibliographical references and index.
    ISBN-10: 0-7660-2455-5
    1. Handicraft—Asia—Juvenile literature. I. Title. II. Series.
TT160.H363 2006
745.5095—dc22

                                    2005027675

ISBN-13: 978-0-7660-2455-7

Printed in the United States of America

10 9 8 7 6 5 4 3

To Our Readers: We have done our best to make sure all Internet Addresses in this book were active and appropriate when we went to press. However, the author and the publisher have no control over and assume no liability for the material available on those Internet sites or on other Web sites they may link to. Any comments or suggestions can be sent by e-mail to comments@enslow.com or to the address on the back cover.

Every effort has been made to locate all copyright holders of material used in this book. If any errors or omissions have occurred, corrections will be made in future editions of this book.

Illustration Credits: Crafts prepared by June Ponte; photography by Lindsay Pries. Corel Corporation, pp. 5, 8, 18, 20; Courtesy of Anne Enslow, p. 4; © 2005 JupiterImages, pp. 13 (photograph in frame).

Cover Illustration: Photography by Lindsay Pries.

Contents

Safety Note: Be sure to ask for help from
               an adult, if needed, to
               complete these crafts!

Introduction

Asian-American crafts were brought to the United States by immigrants from the East. When people from Japan, India, and China came to America, they brought their customs with them. Asian-American customs come from many countries, religions, and traditions.

There are many Asian-American crafts, such as crafts used in storytelling and crafts that are used for decorations. Some crafts make toys, others are for religious ceremonies.

Asian-American crafts existed many years before America was discovered.

This Vietnamese woman is wearing a traditional hat called non.

The dragon dance is an important part of the Chinese New Year.

Over time, these crafts have changed. Other cultures and art have mixed with these crafts. For example, people who make scrapbooks use a form of paper cutting to decorate pages. Paper cutting is a Chinese art form.

Asian-American crafts can be found in stores and craft fairs today. They can also be made from things around the house. Zen gardens and Japanese lanterns can be made from things like shoeboxes and construction paper. Make your own Asian-American crafts.

Kamishibai Story Stage

Before television was invented, Japanese storytellers went from town to town on bicycles. When he got to town, he would set up a wooden theater-shaped box called Kamishibai (kah-mee-she-bye). The storyteller would tell an exciting story with illustrated cards he would put into the Kamishibai. Make your own Kamishibai and tell picture stories to friends.

What You Will Need:

- shoebox
- large index cards
- construction paper
- scissors
- glue
- crayons or markers

1. Place the shoebox on its side. Cut a slot in the top side of your box, all the way from one side to the other.

2. Cover the outside of the box in construction paper. Do not cover the slot. Decorate the outside of the box with crayons, markers, or construction paper. Put the box back on its side with the slotted side up.

3. Choose a favorite story or make up a story. On the index cards, draw pictures that show things that happen in the story. Stack the cards in the order the pictures appear in the story.

4. Drop the first picture into the slot and begin telling the story. Drop pictures into the slot as they come up in the story. The pictures should fall in front of each other so the audience sees each new picture.

1. Cut a Slot in a Shoebox . . .

2. Decorate the Shoebox Stage . . .

3. Draw the cards that will tell your Story . . .

4. Your Stage is ready for Storytelling!

7

Japanese Fan

Living with nature is a part of Japanese culture. Traditional Japanese fans made living with nature easier before air conditioning was invented. People sat outside during summer and used fans to keep cool. Japanese fans are also used for decoration.

What You Will Need:

- poster board or paper plate
- 3 craft sticks
- scissors
- glue
- markers

1. Cut a large circle out of poster board, or use a paper plate.

2. Decorate the circle by writing a story or poem, or by drawing a picture.

3. Glue craft sticks together to make a Y shape.

4. Glue the back of the circle to top of the craft stick Y shape. The bottom of the Y shape is the handle of the fan.

5. Let the glue dry, then use the fan for cooling off or hang it on the wall for decoration.

1. Cut out a large paper circle or use a paper plate . . .

2. Decorate the cirlce by drawing a fan shape on it . . .

3. Glue craft sticks in a "y" and glue them to the back of the paper circle . . .

4. Let your fan dry, and it is ready to use!

Balinese Shadow Puppet

In Bali, shadow plays tell about history and religion. They also tell stories that are funny, sad, or scary. People come to watch these plays for fun, like a movie. Some shadow plays are performed by one person, who works up to twenty puppets.

What You Will Need:

- poster board
- scissors
- pencil
- hole punch
- ½-inch brass fasteners
- 4 nonbendable drinking straws
- clear tape

1. Trace the Balinese shadow puppet patterns onto poster board. (See pages 28–29 for the pattern.)

2. Cut out 4 arm pieces, 2 top leg pieces, 2 bottom leg pieces, and 1 body piece.

3. Punch holes in all the pieces where an X is marked on the pattern. Use brass fasteners to connect the leg pieces together. Connect the arm pieces together, and connect the arms to the top of the body.

4. Color and decorate the puppet as you wish.

5. Tape straws to the ends of legs and arms.

6. Use straws to hold the puppet up and make it dance. Two people may have to work one puppet. Make up stories to act out.

1. Trace the pattern onto poster board . . .

2. Attach the joints of the arms and legs . . .

4. Decorate, and your puppet is ready to dance!

3. Attach the arms and legs to the body . . .

Korean Ornamental Knot Picture Frame

For hundreds of years, the art of knot tying has been passed down in Korea. These knots were used to decorate furniture, clothes, mirrors, and other things. The knots are very hard to learn. There were even knots for brides and knots for religious ceremonies. There were also knots used for bags, spoons, chopsticks, hats, and other everyday items.

What You Will Need:

- colored paper
- 2 large index cards
- scissors
- glue
- pencil

1. Trace the knot pattern onto paper. (See page 26 for the pattern.)

2. Cut an oval from the center of 1 index card.

3. On the other index card, make a line of glue along 3 sides. Do not glue one short side Place the index card with the oval lines-side-down onto the glue. Let dry. A picture can slide into the frame on the side that has not been glued.

4. Decorate the frame by gluing paper knots to the front. Curl the tails of the paper knots, or let them hang down the frame.

5. To make a stand for the frame, fold the oval cut from the index card in half. Glue the oval to the back of the picture frame with the fold at the bottom of frame. Unfold the oval.

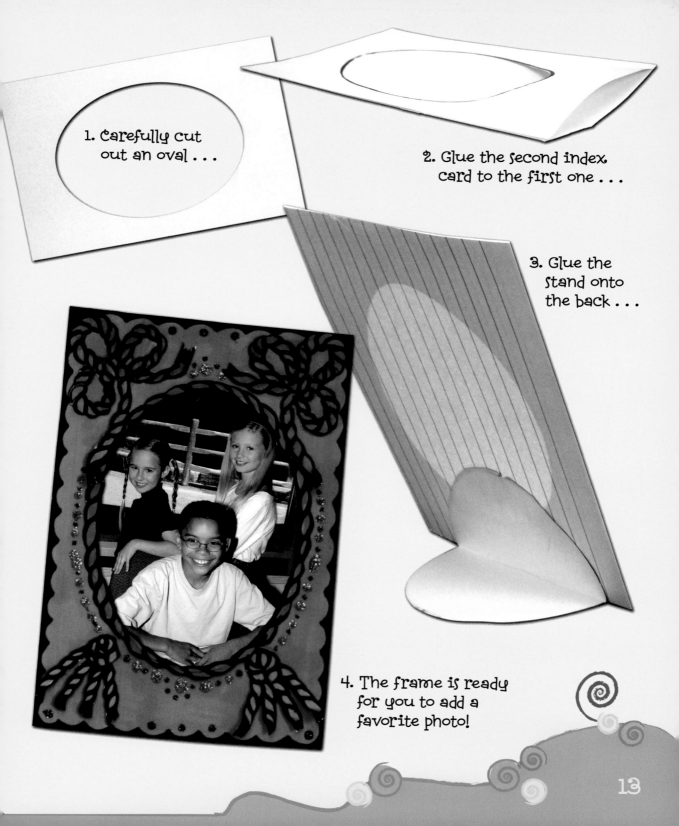

1. Carefully cut out an oval . . .

2. Glue the second index card to the first one . . .

3. Glue the stand onto the back . . .

4. The frame is ready for you to add a favorite photo!

Chinese Paper Cutting

Paper was invented in China, and has been a part of Chinese art ever since. One type of Chinese paper art is paper cutting. Traditional Chinese paper cuts are used to decorate windows, doors, lamps, and gifts. Make your own paper cuts.

What You Will Need:

- pencil
- colored paper
- scissors
- glitter (optional)
- glue (optional)

1. Make a paper cut pattern on white paper. Use any shape you want, or use the pattern on page 26.

2. Carefully trace onto colored paper. Cut it out. Cut out the black shapes on the inside. If you wish, decorate it.

3. Glue to notebooks or binders, or tape to windows and doors.

1. Start with a blank piece of paper . . .

2. Trace a shape, such as a butterfly, onto the paper . . .

3. Cut out and decorate!

Indonesian Theater Mask

In Indonesia, actors wear masks during outdoor theater. The masks are part of the play. Some masks are symbols of gods or creatures. Other masks may show if the character is happy or sad. Make up a play and create masks to go with the story, or make masks to hang on the wall.

What You Will Need:

- paper plate
- puff paint
- markers or poster paint
- scissors
- craft stick
- paint brush

1. Cut out eyes and a mouth from the paper plate.

2. Squeeze puff paint from tube to make lines across mask. Draw a few lines or draw many. Decorate as you want using markers or poster paint. Let paint dry.

3. Glue the craft stick to the bottom of the mask and let dry. Use the mask in a play or hang on the wall.

1. Carefully cut out a face from a paper plate . . .

2. Start to decorate . . .

3. Glue a craft stick to the back . . .

4. Add the finishing touches and your mask is done!

Sand Mandalas

Mandala is a word that means circle. Tibetan monks use sand and paint to make circle designs called mandalas. These designs use many colors and shapes. Mandalas are part of Tibetan religion, and are also pieces of art.

What You Will Need:

- colored sand or glitter
- glue
- poster board
- ruler
- pencil
- paint brush
- paper plate
- clear contact paper

1. Use a plate or other round object to trace a circle on the poster board. Copy the sand mandala pattern into the circle. (See page 27 for the pattern.) Or, make up a different design. Decide what color each piece of the design will be. Lightly write, in pencil, that color in the design.

2. Pour glue onto the paper plate. Use the paint brush to brush glue onto a part of the design. Pour the right color sand or glitter onto that first part of the design. Let the glue dry, then pour extra sand or glitter back into container.

3. Let the design dry overnight. Lay the mandala flat to display. If hanging on a wall, cover the mandala with clear contact paper to keep the sand from falling off.

1. Cut a circle from a piece of poster board . . .

2. Use a ruler to help you draw a design . . .

3. Add glitter or sand and let dry. Your mandala is ready for display!

Emaki

Emaki are scrolls that are read as they are unrolled. A whole book can be written on one scroll. Sometimes, pictures are drawn to go with the story. Make up a story or poem to go in an emaki made with paper and pencils.

What You Will Need:

- 2 unsharpened pencils
- construction paper
- glue
- clear tape
- paint, markers, or crayons

1. Tape 5 pieces of paper together to make one 1 banner.

2. Make a line of glue along the edge of each side of the banner.

3. Press the pencils to the line of glue and let dry.

4. Use paint, markers, or crayons to write a story and draw pictures on the banner.

5. Roll the pencil on the right so the paper wraps around it. Keep rolling until reaching the pencil on the left.

6. Unroll the paper to read the story. Roll up again to carry or put away.

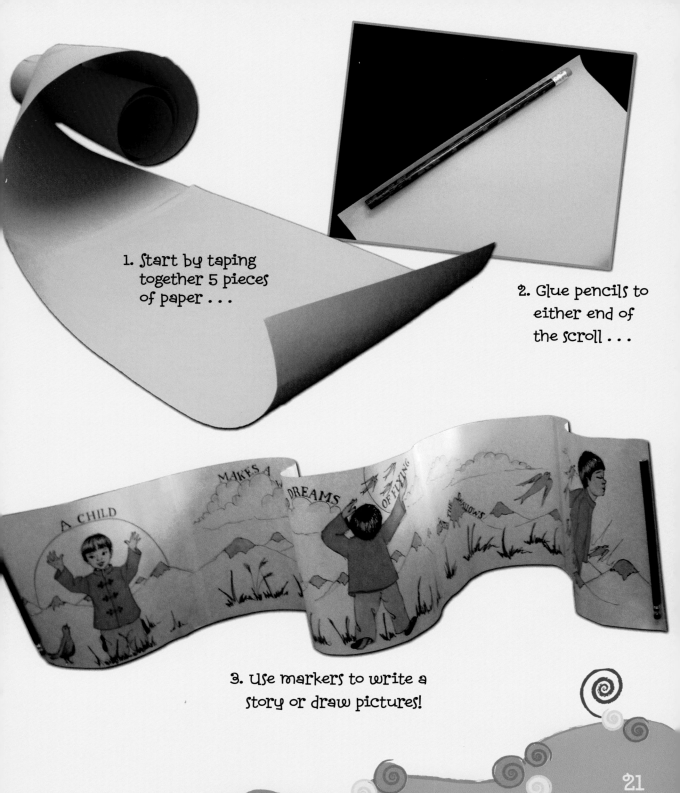

1. Start by taping together 5 pieces of paper . . .

2. Glue pencils to either end of the scroll . . .

3. Use markers to write a story or draw pictures!

A CHILD MAKES A ... DREAMS ... OF FLYING ... SWALLOWS

Hopping Frog

Origami is a Japanese word that means "to fold paper." There are no rules in origami. Paper folding can include using scissors and glue to make shapes of flowers, animals, and people. Try folding paper into shapes and see what things can be made.

What You Will Need:

- paper
- glitter (optional)
- markers (optional)

1. Fold a rectangular piece of paper (½ piece of construction paper) diagonally to make a triangle. Unfold.

2. Fold the paper on the other diagonal to make a triangle. Unfold. There should be an X on the top part of the paper.

3. Fold the paper to make a line through the X.

4. Press the sides of the folds in to make a triangle tent.

5. Take a corner of the triangle and fold it towards the middle. Do the same for the other side.

6. Take the side of the rectangle and fold as shown. Do the same for the other side.

7. Fold the bottom in half to the top.

8. Bend back the piece you just folded. Turn over. Cut half circles into each back leg. Make a "U" shape between the legs to give them shape. Decorate the frog as you wish. Your frog is ready to hop.

Let's get started! Follow the folding steps:

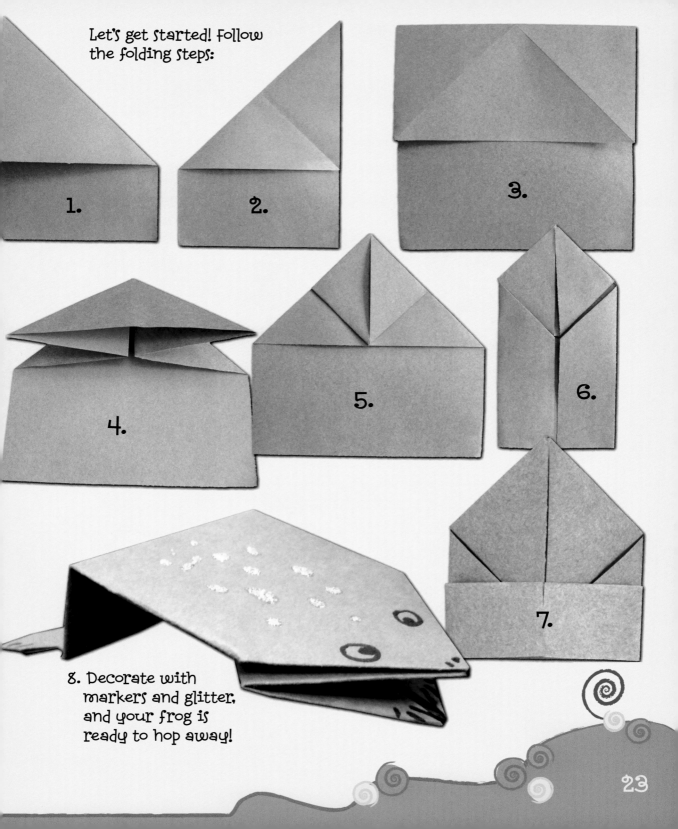

1.

2.

3.

4.

5.

6.

7.

8. Decorate with markers and glitter, and your frog is ready to hop away!

Vietnamese Poster Board Non

A non is a cone-shaped hat worn by many people in Vietnam. There is a village in Vietnam where almost everyone is involved in making these hats. People who visit Vietnam often buy a non to bring home. Make a non to wear when it is sunny outside.

What You Will Need:

- large white poster board
- markers
- scissors
- glue
- yarn
- glitter (optional)

1. Draw a large circle on the poster board. Cut out.
2. Cut a slit in the circle from the edge to the center.
3. Take the left side of the slit and overlap the right side. This creates a cone shape. Glue the poster board down. Let dry.
4. Decorate the cone with markers. Punch holes in opposite edges of the cone. Tie a piece of yarn from one hole to the other.
5. Wear non using yarn to keep the hat from falling off.

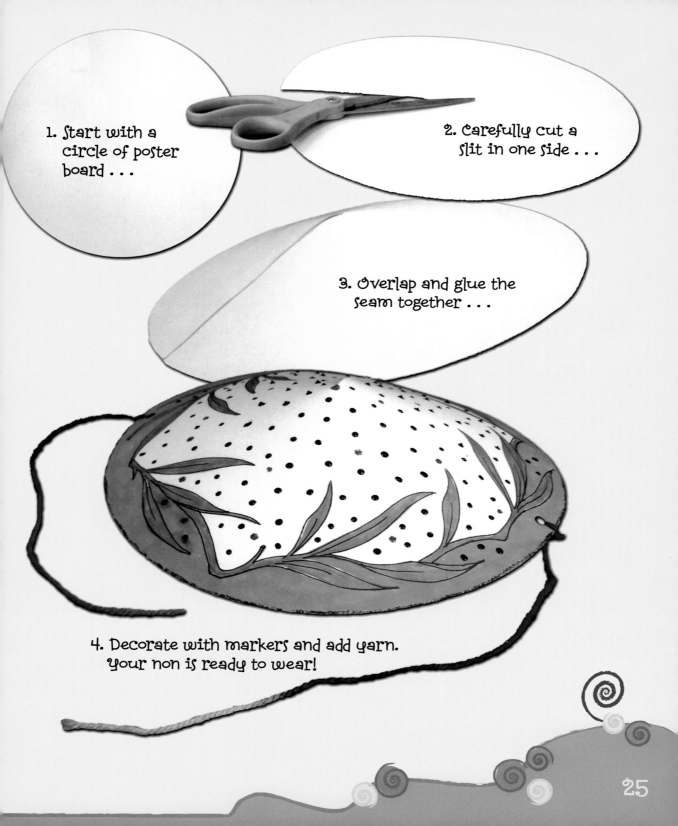

1. Start with a circle of poster board . . .

2. Carefully cut a slit in one side . . .

3. Overlap and glue the seam together . . .

4. Decorate with markers and add yarn. Your non is ready to wear!

Patterns

Use tracing paper to copy the patterns on these pages. Ask an adult to help you cut and trace the shapes onto construction paper.

Use a copier to enlarge or shrink the design to the size you want.

knot frame

At 100%

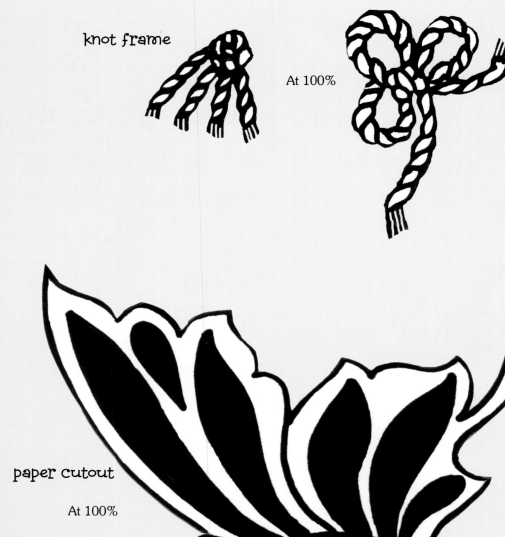

paper cutout

At 100%

Mandala

Enlarge by 165%

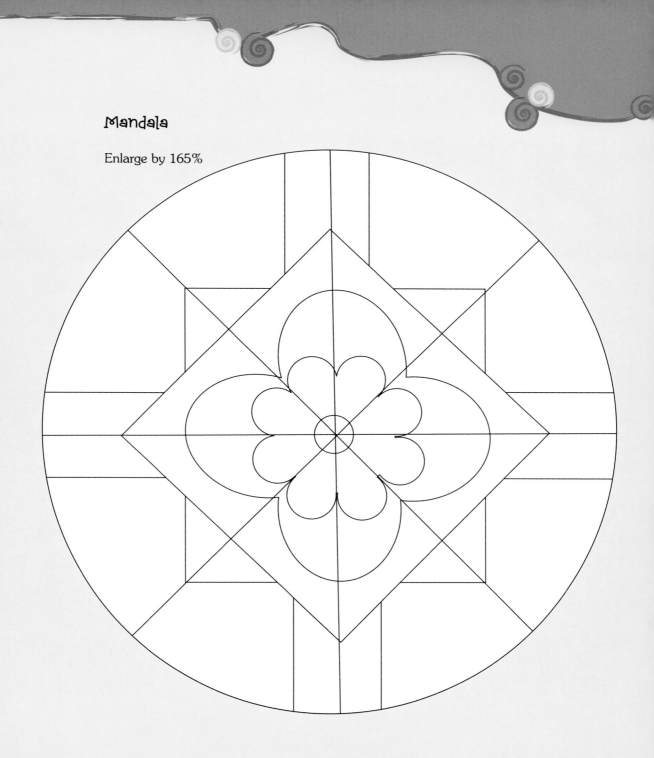

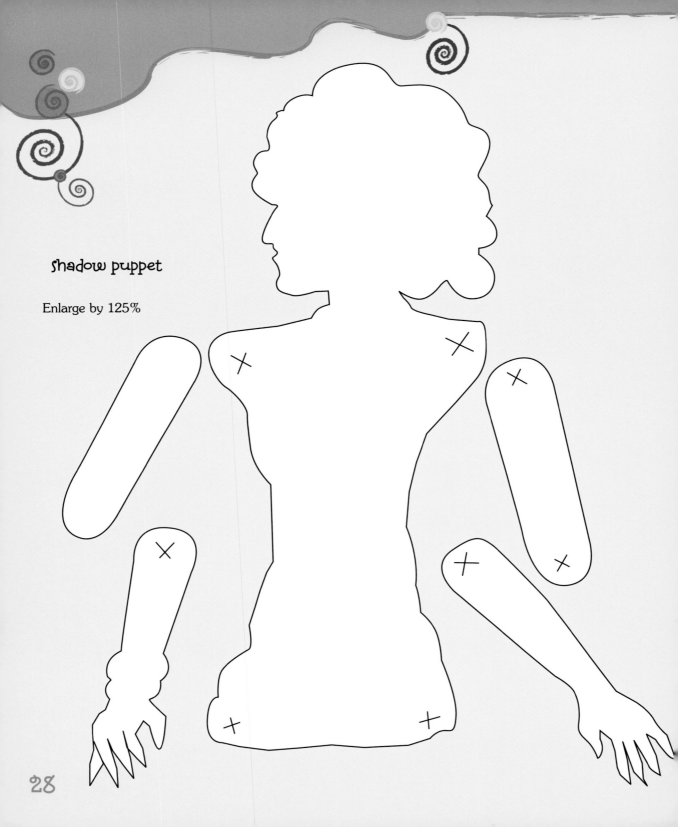

shadow puppet

Enlarge by 125%

28

Enlarge by 125%

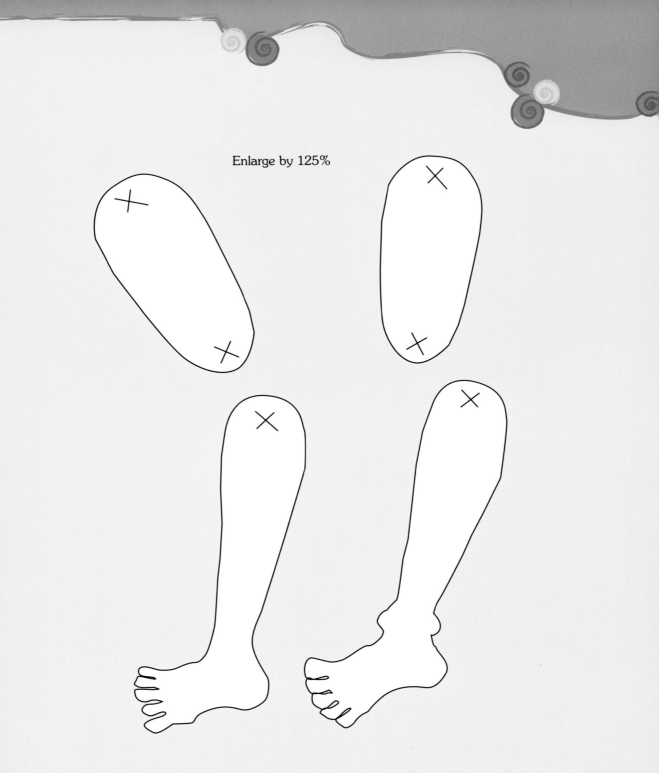

Reading About

Books

Chin-Lee, Cynthia. *A is for Asia*. New York: Orchard Books, 1997.

Coppendale, Jean. *Special Days and Holidays*. Chrysalis Education/Smart Apple Media, 2003.

Grahame, Deborah. *Asia*. Chanhassen, Minn.: Child's World, 2004.

Guile, Melanie. *Culture in North & South Korea*. Chicago, Ill.: Raintree, 2004.

Kalman, Bobbie. *Vietnam: The Culture*. New York: Crabtree Publishing. Co., 2002.

Simonds, Nina, Leslie Swartz, and the Children's Museum of Boston. *Moonbeams, Dumplings, & Dragon Boats: A Treasury of Chinese Holiday Tales, Activities & Recipes*. San Diego, Calif.: Harcourt, Inc., 2002.

Terzian, Alexandra M. *The Kids' Multicultural Art Book: Arts & Craft Experiences from Around the World*. Milwaukee, Wisc.: Gareth Stevens, 1999.

Internet Addresses

Korean American Museum

<http://www.kamuseum.org>

Learn more about the Korean American culture.

The Mandala Project

<http://www.mandalaproject.org>

Learn more about Mandalas.

Wayang Kulit: The Ancient Shadow Plays of Bali

<http://www.tunasmekar.org/WayKul.html>

Read about shadow plays.

Index.